Minnette Slayback-Carper

The Dance of Death

And Other Stories

Minnette Slayback-Carper

The Dance of Death
And Other Stories

ISBN/EAN: 9783337005214

Printed in Europe, USA, Canada, Australia, Japan

Cover: Foto ©Thomas Meinert / pixelio.de

More available books at **www.hansebooks.com**

THE DANCE OF DEATH.

AND OTHER STORIES.

BY
MINNETTE
SLAYBACK-
CARPER.

THE DANCE OF DEATH.

AND OTHER STORIES.

BY

MINNETTE SLAYBACK-CARPER.

With Illustrations by the Author.

BUXTON & SKINNER, PUBLISHERS,
ST. LOUIS, MO.
1894.

CONTENTS:

THE DANCE OF DEATH.

It was in the good old times at Paris. There is no city like Paris. One can be a thorough bohemian, and a society man at the same time. Thus, then, I lived. I knew men among the artists and poets and actors, and was intimate with exquisites of the highest aristocracy. My parents were rich. My life was spent in one ceaseless search after pleasure. I loved many times. I had seen beautiful women, proud and noble, whom men worshipped. I worshipped also. I was young and impetuous; the women always liked me; but I gave my heart up entirely when I met La Joie.

It was one evening when I had gone to the opera with my friend Julien Enterre, the mysterious, the beautiful. No one had ever been in his lodgings, that we knew of. His valet was allowed only in the dressing cabinet. We penetrated as far as the smoking room, and a tiny place he called the study—a fascinating nook, hung with pale

silks and containing rare bits of water-color painting and dainty china. We were never asked to
go farther—not even I, his good friend. Enterre
fairly lived at the theatre of evenings, but went
always alone. After the play he quickly disappeared. I suspected him of many things, but he
had been away from Paris for so long, that our
acquaintance was compelled a new start. This
evening he had asked me to accompany him and
I consented to go. We sat in perfect seats in the
stalls. I had been gazing at friends in the boxes,
and was whispering in Enterre's ear, when he
suddenly said:

"Hush! The ballet, and La Joie!"

His manner was too excited to escape notice.
Then I looked at the stage. The beautiful crea-
ture dancing was perfectly formed beyond dreams.
She was young, one could see, with an exquisite
face, and neck and arms like a Venus; and as her
gauzy skirts dipped up and down around her, she
danced with grace unexcelled. The stalls were full
of men. When she finished, she blew a kiss and
indulged in a fleeting smile that seemed to caress
the whole audience. Yet it appeared to my conceited fancy, that she looked in my direction for

just a passing second longer than in another. There was a storm of applause, which brought her tripping back to the footlights. They were not content with her merely bowing, however, so the music began, and she repeated the swaying movements that were the very poetry of motion.

A full pink rosebud decorated Enterre's coat lapel. At the end of the dance he extracted this, and flung it upon the stage. It fell at her feet amongst bouquets and other roses, but she picked out Enterre's rose and kissed it toward the audience. Julien stood.

"Come!" he said, "She will not dance again. It is near the end."

I was not at all willing to depart, but being Enterre's guest, I followed him as he went out.

"Would you care to meet her?" he asked outside. "Come, I will take you. She has the most enjoyable little suppers. You will find there Delrois and Leblanc—others too, who think she is beautiful and witty. One night you may forego your foolish society lounging."

"My dear Enterre," I said. "Nothing pleases me better than the prospect. If you will assure me of a welcome."

"You are my friend," he answered simply.

I accompanied him gladly enough. Mademoiselle had not yet arrived from the theatre when we reached her apartments, but would soon return. The room that we were ushered into was a charming one which no money had been spared to make beautiful. Enterre strode up to a small picture that hung rather back from observation, and stood there long, looking at it. I approached, and saw over his shoulder that it was a young married couple in their honeymoon. My friend turned away with a quick sigh.

"What is the matter, Enterre?" I cried, clapping him upon the back. "You are so queer of late."

"Yes, I am queer—of late," he said.

Two other men came in, both of whom we knew. Then rose the sound of much laughter and many voices. Enterre stood at a table turning over the leaves of a book.

"Enterre," I whispered, "I do not know La Joie."

"True," he laughed, "and she is very particular about having people presented."

And then the door opened, and she entered, fol-

lowed by a great crowd of gentlemen, and not
another woman in sight but her maid. She wore
a long carriage cloak, which she presently threw
off, leaving, to my surprise, only her ballet costume with its short fluffy skirts and pink tights. I
was duly presented, and then merely watched her
as she sat in a big chair chatting busily with the
crowd of men about her. There were at least
fifteen of them scattered around the room, most
of them grouped near La Joie. Of the remaining
few who talked among themselves, I remember
Enterre was one. He apparently listened to a
man with long hair and a bright face. In reality
his thoughts were with La Joie, as she merrily
laughed and conversed. He occasionally glanced
at her with such a light in his eyes as only accom-
panies fervent love. Enterre bewitched by the
ballet-dancer! At the time I thought how foolish
it was.

This same danseuse, however, was able to keep
those men at her side in fascinated attention until
supper was announced. Then, with wild mirth
they escorted her into the adjoining room, and sat
them down. There was no lavish extravagance
in the supper, with the exception of the wines.

The wine was always the same, they told me, and Mlle. La Joie did not pay for it. It was sent to her as a friendly present, always anonymously. One of the toasts, I remember, was to the wine; and then to the giver of the wine. La Joie herself proposed the latter. I noticed she did not drink much. One glass was slowly sipped during the meal. She made up for it in gay speeches that flashed from her sweet lips as champagne bubbles from the bottom of the glass.

"Now, Mademoiselle, will you dance?" said one.

There was a great clamor then, a rattling of glassware, and noisy cries. They rose to their feet and bore away the dishes from the table, piling them pell-mell in a corner of the room, and the cloth at the top. Mademoiselle motioned to a musical genius, who disappeared in the next room, and soon the piano answered to his fingers the gayest strains. Smiling, so that her fine white teeth sparkled between her parted lips, La Joie sprang upon the long table, and there danced. I shall never forget. It was better than the stage dancing, for here one could see her face and its bright expression, and view well the toes as they flashed about on the dark wood. Now her slender

body curved and swayed like a tall poplar tossed
by the wind; now she spun about till the short
skirts were horizontal, and now—she made a
mocking bow and ceased, and sat upon the table
laughing. She was beautiful then. Her hair was
blue-black, her skin pale, she was peculiar in that
she would use no cosmetiques—no rouge. Her
eyes were a clear, pure grey, with no blue about
them, but they were eyes that spoke. Her mouth
was exquisite; her chin such that one longed to
take it in one's hand, and beneath the chin, at the
throat was a heavenly place for a kiss. She smiled
at me when she saw me dart forward with the rest,
and with that smile she won my allegiance, as I
knew she had conquered that of Enterre and many
others. I flung care to the winds. "The others"
might go,—I could find another to take Enterre's
place, but there was not a second La Joie.

Enterre and I were the last ones to leave that
night; we lingered for a moment after the rest
had gone. She was very friendly to Enterre in a
charming, frank way, so that a little green spot
burned up in my heart. I managed to whisper
and ask what were her favorite flowers.

"I shall not tell you," she laughed back. "But

if you desire to be foolish, you may send me crimson roses."

I looked across the room to a cabinet where in a white bowl, a great mass of violets lay. She saw my glance. She looked first at me, then at Enterre, a spirit of mischief in her eyes; then she crossed the room and pressed a kiss upon the blue flowers. Enterre turned away, his face crimson.

"How angry he grows," I thought. "Shall I ever be so foolish over her, I wonder?"

We made our adieus and went as far as the street when Enterre cried hastily:

"Wait a moment," and returned up the staircase. He kept me for some time waiting. I paced up and down the pavement, going over all her guests, endeavoring to trace the sender of the violets. When at last he appeared there was a bunch of violets in his lapel, and on his face a look I had never seen before. I warn you to be watchful of such beautiful men.

To say that I went to the theatre often, after that, would but faintly intimate the manner in which I haunted the footlights. Night after night found me at the play, and with but little trouble I could always discover Enterre. We spoke more coldly. I now attended La Joie's little suppers by myself. There was always a joyous crowd of young men at them, always the mysterious and fascinating, delicious wines; always the bowl of fresh violets, and always Enterre stayed latest. I fell madly in love. I repaired to La Joie's every night and felt a craving desire to strangle my friend and to dash the bowl of blue flowers upon the hearth. Enterre only grew more beautiful and more distrait as the days passed. A settled melancholy filled his eyes, and enhanced their sweet expression, but La Joie seemed to notice him less and less.

I often passed Mademoiselle's lodgings in the day-time. One day late in the forenoon I saw her, accompanied by a maid, issue forth with her arms full of flowers. Among them I felt sure were the red roses I had ordered for her that morning. I had often sent them, but they were never visible in her apartments. Now I followed as she walked rapidly up the street to a poor-looking house, which she entered. I waited in the cafe till she re-appeared—empty-handed.

"We shall see," I said.

2

When she was once again inside her own door, I returned across the street to the shabby tenement. I knocked as I had seen Mademoiselle do. A feeble voice from within said: "Entrez," and I entered a small, dark room. A pale child sat huddled up in pillows, and in his hands and in a vase upon the table were roses—red, white and pink—a wealth of them.

"Was that Mlle. La Joie who was just here, my little one?" I asked.

"Is that her name, Monsieur?" asked the child in return. "She would never tell me. La Joie. It suits her. She has just given me much happiness. She often brings me flowers. Best of all I love the red roses. She tells me she does not bring all she has, but she shares equally with me. She has many flowers—and oh! she is so beautiful! She must be glad to live."

"Poor little man, so she is," I said. I dropped a coin down upon the pillow, and went quickly from the room.

That afternoon, Pantreaux, one of the men who were frequently at La Joie's suppers, came to me with a plan. We were to go to the theatre that evening, each with our favorite flower pinned on his coat, roses preferred.   At the end of La Joie's dance we were to rain the blossoms upon her. There were many in the secret.

The evening came.   I wore a rose with a color like blood.   Enterre sat near me.   His button-hole held two buds—one pink, the other white.   I wondered at this—my curiosity was always like a woman's.

La Joie danced as she never had before.   It was in a most eccentric fancy named "The Dance of Death."   Her tights were black, the low-cut bodice and the filmy skirts.   Her black hair was in keeping with the toilette.   The chorus was also in black; but who heeded the chorus?   When her dance ceased, lo! from a hundred hands came as many roses and more—red and white, pink and yellow, they fell about her, and she stood swaying and laughing at the charge.   And then she stooped and picked up something that glistened as she raised it.   She kissed it and thrust it in her black hair.   It was a silver arrow shot through a bunch of violets.   Who had thrown it?   I looked at Enterre.   He was leaning forward, the white rose remained in his lapel—the pink one lay un-

heeded at the feet of La Joie. He, too, had seen
the arrow and the violets.

La Joie was twice recalled to dance and refused
a third time on account of fatigue. Then, joined
by Enterre, I hurried out and proceeded to the
apartments of the danseuse. There were already
many there, assembled for the coming gayety.
Later they poured in until the rooms were crowded
with a good natured throng that chatted and
laughed and moved about. At last a commotion
near the door heralded her approach, and the con-
course of men shouted "Vive La Joie" until the
roof rang. Her hands were full of rosebuds, and
her bright, beautiful face sparkled with pleasure.
Willing slaves unclasped the long cloak she wore,
and as its hood fell from her head, we noticed the
silver arrow and the bunch of violets in her hair.

"Oh! An arrow, Mademoiselle! Is that what
it was. I could not see," said Leblanc.

"Yes,—it is an arrow—a silver arrow," she
answered. She took it from the dark meshes with
difficulty, and laughed. "Friends, this is a warning! Yes, what I say, I mean. It is a warning.
Once before I received one—a dagger that time,
with a silver hilt, and upon it the identical motto

that this bears. See, here engraved—'Prenez garde.' It was the dance of death, to-night. Perchance this arrow points to my—"

"Mademoiselle!" cried Enterre—"What ails you? Sad? In such brilliant company? It is a warning, surely, but a warning that all may read. It means that where so many adore you there must be jealousy, and where there is jealousy, anger crops out, and anger produces quarreling; quarreling breeds duels—and sometimes death ensues."

He was leaning over the back of her chair—she turning around to look up at his handsome, boyish face. Between his closed teeth, under cover of the laugh which went around, he spoke something quickly and softly, so that only she could hear. She let her breath come out sharply, and turning to Pantreaux, disdained Enterre. It was a strange evening all through. When Mademoiselle first came in she had shaken hands with every one. After that I did not approach her. I talked with artists of painting; discussed music with composers; literature and society with their respective representatives. Once, as I lounged from one group to another, a maid opened the

door to an adjoining apartment, and I saw into
La Joie's bedroom.   It was the daintiest chamber
imaginable, and was furnished in white, blue and
gold.   The little brass bedstead was draped in
white; over the low, broad dressing table was a
large square mirror framed in white, and upon a
stand near by, was a flower vase holding a quantity
of glowing carmine roses.   They were my roses!
My heart leaped into my throat.   My arteries
tried to burst.   I was at once ice-cold and red-hot.
My companions chaffed me on my sudden acces-
sion of color.   I shook them off and made
towards where La Joie held forth in vivacious con-
verse to a huddled group of men.

"Does she never grow tired of talking?" I asked
of Enterre, standing upon the edge.

"Yes—she wearies of it.   It tires her to entertain them, but she knows it pleases—so she does
it."   He shrugged his shoulders as though to say
he could do nothing, and moved away.   "It is her
duty as hostess of a salon," he said, as he went.
He was sarcastic, and apparently in a bad mood.
Poor Enterre!   Was it with a secret feeling of
exultation that I said to myself, "He has had his
day!"

There was no regular supper, that night. Ices were served, and champagne, an innovation; but they implored La Joie to dance her little conceit upon the table. La Joie did not always dance for us. On the nights when she came home clad in ordinary evening dress we had no dancing. On such occasions I thought her most charming. I grew fastidious. So being now costumed a la ballet, they were at liberty to request her to favor them, and she consented. The table was accordingly drawn to the middle of the floor, and willing hands assisted her to lightly leap upon it. The piano music began, and La Joie danced. But lo, as she tripped about upon the inadequate space, the silver arrow which she had replaced, dropped from her hair to the table, and rebounded, Enterre catching it. Mademoiselle suddenly ceased, and all pale, held out her hand for the mysterious trifle. Enterre, looking straight into her eyes, seized the hand and kissed it, leaving the arrow in her clasp.

Cries of "Go on—proceed—encore," resounded, but Mademoiselle refused. She sat upon the edge of the table apparently much disturbed—tears filled her eyes and brought forth exclamations and protests.

"I am afraid," she said, shaking her head.   "It is the dance of death, you know."

And all their laughter could not move her. Enterre suddenly left the assembly, and did not return.   It much surprised but gladdened me. Now would be my opportunity.   Now I should speak.   I patiently lingered until the last devoted man had gone.

"La Joie," I began softly.

She turned a bit pale; a tremor, of nervousness, perhaps, passed over her.

"Henri," she said, quickly.   "Do you go, too. Depart, I pray you.   I am very tired—I require rest.   I beg of you go."

"When, then, may I speak?" I asked.

"If I live," she said slowly, "and am here—to-morrow."

"Morbid one," I said.

"Go, now," she cried—"at once."

I obeyed, but stopped in the cafe opposite, to buy a cigar.   As I came out and reached the shadow, I noticed a man going in La Joie's doorway.   It was Enterre; I saw him plainly.   What did it mean?   A biting jealousy possessed me, and I waited for his return to the street.   He was

not long gone, and when he reappeared, he was
wiping off his waistcoat with a handkerchief.
Evidently she had bestowed more violets, and he
was brushing off the water that had fallen from
their stems.

"Well," I reasoned, "she gave them to him to be
quickly rid of his presence. To-morrow will prove
her."

I slept but little that night. I lay awake mus-
ing of the morning, wondering how we should
both behave, and I rose comparatively early and
went to my florist. He was rich in apologies, for
he had not a single red rose in the house. When
one is in love, trifles do not worry.

"It does not matter," I said, lightly. "Give me
white ones." I picked out a great bunch of the
slender-budded, transparent Nephites.

It was about twelve o'clock as I reached the
domicile of Mademoiselle. I paused on the step.
A thousand conflicting emotions seized me. I
thought of her fears and forebodings of the previous night. This life did not befit her. I would
make her my wife; together we would go far away
from gay, tiring Paris, and begin a new existence.
Then I resolutely demanded admittance. The

door was opened by a maid whose eyes were red from recent weeping.

"Oh! Monsieur," she cried, bursting into fresh tears, "I implore you, do not come in!"

"What has happened, Marie?" I asked.

"I—oh! Really I have not the heart to tell. Last night Mademoiselle La Joie gave me permission to spend it with my parents, and this morning when I returned to assist Mademoiselle with her dressing—I find her—oh! Mon Dieu— as you shall see."

She hurriedly ascended the stairs, and I bounded up.

"But Monsieur," said Marie, "you will not enter the room?"

"What is it," I gasped. "For God's sake, tell me."

"See for yourself," said the woman.

We were at the door of the dining salon. Marie opened the portal, and—I saw. Upon the dark table lay a still figure. It was La Joie, yet clad in her dancing costume of black; her fair, bare arms gleaming white against the sombre color of the dress; her face was pale; the arrow shone in her hair. But something gave color to one fair

THE DANCE OF DEATH. 27

hand and brightened the black satin bodice—
something red like my usual roses. You have
guessed; it was blood from her young heart, drawn
forth by a small dagger which had entered the
source of her life and banished its spirit.

"Do not touch her, Monsieur," cried Marie.
"The authorities must see the body as it is."

Disregarding this, I dragged myself forward
and gazed at the quiet, calm, dead face, with its
closed eyes, and then at the horrid wound and its
silver-headed cause. The dagger I examined, re-
membering her words of the night before. Upon
the hilt was engraved, "Prenez garde," and below,
in small letters, "Enterre."

"Mon Dieu!" I screamed, "Enterre! Enterre."

Like a fiend with rage, I tore the wrappings
from my flowers. I kissed her white forehead
and scattered over her the roses not less white,
some of which fell upon the cruel wound. I
rushed from the house. I burned for revenge—
Enterre—Enterre had done the deed. The
authorities had been informed of the murder, so I
went straightway to Enterre's dwelling house. I
gave his valet no time to announce me. I brushed

past him into the master's sleeping chamber, and there found him I sought.

He was seated facing me, with wild, sleepless eyes, and a countenance haggard and stricken.

"You have heard?" he asked.

"I have seen your cowardly work. Assassin!"

He stared at me in an emotionless way, and seemed so broken and resistless, that, contrary to my first impetuous intentions, I did not rush forward and grip the breath from his throat.

"Enterre, in God's name—did you do this thing?"

"You refer to La Joie's death, I presume," he slowly said. "Yes, I did it—with these hands. See, I have not yet washed the stain from my fingers."

He had not risen from his chair, but turned his hands so that I might see the damning evidence.

"Enterre," I said, "you have gone mad."

"No," he replied, sadly. "I have not lost my mind. Would to heaven I had. I have not slept at all this night past, Henri, but I sat up, and wrote to you a short history of my life. I had not thought to see you again, old friend."

He rose, and took from the table a large

envelope which he handed to me, and which bore my name. Then he walked to his dressing table. Before I knew what he would do, he had raised a pistol from the table, and by the aid of the mirror, had fired into his breast. He did not speak again. Assistance was of no avail.

———————

As you may imagine, these events had no trifling effect upon me, and although I played a very prominent part in the testimony for the investigation, I was hardly able to stand. It was some time before I had sufficient command over my nerves to read the packet Julien Enterre had given me. When at length I felt willing to see the poor fellow's secret, it was upon the ocean steamer, on my way to America. The papers contained about what I shall say.

He had gone to the United States several years before, and in New Orleans had met a young girl of excellent French family—whom I afterwards knew as La Joie. He fell deeply in love with her, and having the love reciprocated, but being objected to by the young lady's people, he had persuaded her to elope with him, and they were married. Fortune, fickle jade that she is, had left them almost destitute in New York. Enterre, having quarreled with his father, dared ask no money from France. Having been unaccustomed to labor, he could find only insufficiently paying employment. To support themselves they both must work, and La Joie went upon the stage. Three years of it had made her a fine ballet dancer. Then Enterre's father died, leaving Julien independent—provided he married a cousin. They came back to France. Julien accepted the money, and had apparently been reconciled to marrying the cousin. But he made her angry by his indifference, and her parents finding a richer husband for the beautiful girl, Monsieur Enterre was left with his money in peace. La Joie had, in the meantime, been harassed with anxiety about Enterre. She had left the stage and was living in the apartments which Enterre occupied. But a misunderstanding of affairs, a fear lest he would repudiate her, caused her to seek a position as danseuse in Paris. She had never again relinquished this, although Julien implored her to do so, and assured her that he had never held aught but honorable intentions

towards her—his true wife. The engagement with
his cousin had been but a ruse to obtain money.
By this time, however, she had become acquainted
with many men, and, growing capricious, had
made Enterre promise that for a time at least, he
would not divulge their marriage. He was with
her constantly; he sent the wines; he gave the
violets; he always remained until the last caller
had departed. He loved and guarded her always.
She had promised that if he would allow her to
score certain triumphs, she would cease her stage
life, and be all to him that a wife should be. The
success she begged was obtained, and he threw
the dagger at her feet. She still delayed. A second time he threw the arrow. Then she told him
that she still loved him, but she loved fame and
the stage better. If he accepted her as his wife, it
would be on condition that she might continue
her stage career. I will give you Enterre's remaining words. They seem burned into my
brain.

"I looked at her, so fair, so young and so cruel.
I foresaw the future and what her existence would
become. I viewed my own desolation. I had
spoken in vain. I went to the cabinet under pre-

tense of smelling the violets placed there—my violets whose emblem was 'faithfulness.' In reality, I took from it the dagger which I had given her; and returning to where she sat upon the table—swinging her feet in and out, looking too perfect to die, but too pure to become corrupt, I thrust the knife into her heart. She only lived to breathe my miserable name; then I laid her upon the table, closed her eyes and kissed them close—and may God rest her sweet soul."

MISS KEMBALL.

"What a wretch you are, Mr. Anson!" and little Miss Blake's blue eyes were full of reproach as she said it. "I have asked you a question three times."

"I beg pardon, Miss Blake, ask it again," he said, bending over her as she sat, and he stood, in a crowded ball room.

"I asked who is that tall girl over there in light blue?"

"She is a Miss Ernai Kemball," he answered.

"Do you know her? Ernai—what an odd name!"

"I have never been presented," he said to her question.

"I should lose no time in getting acquainted if I were a man," said Miss Blake. "The men seem to go crazy over her."

"They do," Carl assented.

"You are very indifferent, do you know?" she asked.

"So I have been told."

"Really, though, Mr. Anson, wouldn't you like to meet Miss Kemball?"

"I should be delighted, truly. I have a desire to look well at her eyes. They say she has most beautiful eyes. Why, do you know, Briggs (I get all my information from Briggs)—Briggs wrote a sonnet to her eyes. Oh! yes, I should be happy to meet her."

"Why don't you say it as though you meant it? You are the most indifferent man I ever saw," she laughed. "Why not have Mr. Briggs introduce you?"

"Oh! Dear me, Miss Blake! Poor Briggs has too many would-be-successful rivals already. No, not Briggs, decidedly."

"She is a very fortunate girl," breathed Miss Blake, thinking of Ernai's popularity.

"In not having to meet me?" said Carl, smiling. "Thanks."

"It did sound that way, didn't it? But you know what I meant."

"Yes."

"Ah! here comes Tom Haddon. We must part. I trust you will meet the fair beauty." And nodding and smiling, not meaning a word of her wish, she glided away upon the arm of her partner.

Carl Anson remained standing where she had left him. Celia was desperately in love with him —every one knew that, with the exception, perhaps, of himself. But most of the girls were smitten with him; he was a favorite puzzle and source of aggravation to them. He did not dance; would not,—for he was well able to "trip the light fantastic toe,"—and generally stayed with the wall-flowers; or if any one were willing he sat out the dances with them. They were always willing to have his name on their cards, whether he danced or walked, or listened in a fascinatingly unconscious way to their chatter. It was accepted that a wager was the cause of his abstinence, for a year back he had danced as willingly as the next man. But Carl was changed in every way, his friends said. At the club he was only half a good fellow, where he had formerly led the van. Something was the cause. Money troubles it could not possibly be, as he was of wealth enough to be considered one of the great catches. They did not for a moment suspect him of being in love. He never seemed to care for

one woman's society more than another's, and
love was out of the fashion, and decidedly not
Anson's style.

He stood this evening, with very thoughtful
eyes looking at Ernai Kemball.

"Poor fools!" he mused, at sight of the men
gathered about her. "What will it ever profit
them to be throwing their hearts away upon her?
She will play them all, and at the last take the
one with most money."

Mr. Anson had not himself been so treated,
but a marriage in a relative's case had proved to
be founded upon the wealth of one, and the beauty
of the other, and consequently had not had the
happiest result in the world.

Carl's ideas of marriage and love were unusual
for a society man. He often wished he were poor
that he might be loved for himself—if he were
worth loving. He did not care for his handsome
face; he did not believe his deep grey eyes were
beautiful, nor his mouth simply perfect. He persuaded himself that a conceited man was a fool,
and tried to live up to his idea. But argue with
himself as he might, he was the handsomest man
on the floor that night, just as in his eyes, Ernai

Kemball was the loveliest—nay, the one beautiful
woman.

He amused Ernai beyond measure. She had
known him by sight for a year, and was aware
that he had known her face before that. And yet
he would not be introduced. She hesitated between anger and amusement for awhile, glided
into the latter, and waited.

He had crossed a street once, down which her
cart was being carried at a break-neck pace, by
a horse who was too frightened to heed her hand
or voice. He had run in front of the animal,
grasped the rein, and brought it to a quivering
halt. It was not a runaway, but it might have
been, and Ernai had poured out her thanks in a
way that she seldom allowed herself; and she had
been most generous with a grateful glance from
her no longer languid eyes. But he had lifted
his hat, and passed on through the gaping crowd
which always gathers in the twinkling of an eye
around an excitement upon the street. He had
never presumed to take the least advantage,
nor had he requested to know her. But—she
waited.

She was upon Briggs' arm when Carl was gazing at her so intently, and when, turning, she looked straight into his eyes, she said to Briggs:

"I have a desire to meet your friend, Mr. Anson. I think he will never ask to be presented to me, but, in Pity's name, appear to introduce us by accident."

"With pleasure," said Briggs, to whom her word was law. "We shall pass by; I shall have something very important to say to him, and shall ask you if you will be so kind as to stop with me. You will give a reluctant consent; we shall stop, you be introduced, and I tell him my nonsense. Then you may absorb him in conversation. I'll bet you can draw him out, Miss Kemball. He's been locked up in himself for a year or more. Conceited? No! No one less so, but er-er-taciturn, you know."

"Yes, I understand. There he is."

It was done. The innocent Carl felt his heart beat up into his throat as he bowed. He heard Briggs' voice; returned an answer to his question, and through it all, could retain no word of it. He afterwards learned that Briggs had made an appointment with him, and was full of wrath because Anson did not keep it. But Carl remem-

bered every slightest syllable that Ernai spoke.
He remembered, too, a vow he had once taken;
that he would never joyfully meet another woman
until he had met Ernai Kemball; that he would
never dance with a girl until he danced with her.

"Have you a dance for me, Miss Kemball?" he
asked.

For answer she drew her pencil through the
name opposite a waltz, and gave the waltz to him.
"It is very wicked," she said, "but I will do it."
And she made the disappointed one believe he
had displeased her in some way to merit its being
taken from him.

And there was no longer an indifferent look
on Carl's face as he waited for his dance. He
went to her with a glad heart, and tried to be as
composed as he had been when he leaned against
the wall, but succeeded only in obtaining the out-
ward semblance of self-possession.

She was very beautiful, indeed, he thought, and
her waltzing finished him. He had at last looked
into her eyes—deep, lustrous, brown ones, nearly
on a level with his own; and he was six feet in
his stockings. Let me tell you, though, that
looking he had lost his heart. Her hair was a

bright brown with glints of gold in the high-
lights, and her black lashes curled upwards with
a sweep which enhanced the glances she could
give. Her mouth was tender, loving, and very
kissable; the chin firmly, delicately moulded.

She had small white hands with round, tapering,
pink-tipped fingers, at this time covered by the
jealous gloves; dainty feet that hardly seemed in
keeping with her tall, graceful body; and as
though Fortune had not cared to stint meet cov-
erings for such a glorious figure, Ernai had all the
money, and therefore all of the clothes she desired.

It was easy to fall in love with Ernai Kemball,
but she was so coolly, lazily indifferent, that to
make love was quite as difficult as to fall in love
was easy; and such a thing as winning her heart
seemed out of the question.

She was not a flirt in the ordinary acceptation
of the term, but she appeared to have no desire
for earnest devotion. She gave one no chance
to put in a tender little speech, and if one made
it in spite of her, she looked at him in an amused
sort of way, that fairly drove a sensitive man to
despair.

But without exertion or endeavor she was the most popular girl one could name. The laziest men in society, whom other women vainly fussed over to draw out, threw aside their habitual willingness to lie back and be amused, and made strenuous efforts to entertain her; and now Anson, who was considered utterly callous and indifferent, awoke to the fact that his heart was not the passive organ he had imagined it. But he vowed she should not know it, nor should she have it entirely, until he thought she loved him. Poor girl, she had the name of being a flirt, and he had often heard of her victims. Anson opined Briggs to be of the latter, and with him as an example, was cautious.

He danced with her once again, and before the beauty left, had obtained permission to call. Indifferent until now, henceforth he would be second to none in pursuit of his happiness.

Briggs took him first, it happened. She wore a light, soft silk, that had a shimmer, and the faintest possible perfume about it, and she leaned back in her chair fascinating Briggs by her attention as he told some stories that were not perfectly true.

She rarely looked at Anson—to his disgust. It was one of her ways of flirting, of course, he argued, and he would not fall in love with her— when he was too far fallen to obtain rescue. Once, after one of Briggs' efforts, she, giving a low laugh as tribute to the story, fluttered one glance into Carl's eyes that made his heart go double its ordinary speed.

After that it was an easy down-hill road. He came often at her invitation or without it and wore his heart out looking at her and hearing her low, perfectly distinct voice. But she was cold as ice, calm, queenly, with never so much as a look to encourage him, till he was bound to acknowledge that she was no mere coquette. Being hard to win, men loved her and for herself, and he grew jealous of her power. Was there nothing in him to love? Did he have nothing but his money to make him eligible? He hated it, but was glad that, having it, he was enabled to be with her. If she loved now—if she could love him, it would not be for money, surely—surely.

The slow changes of a year found him more her slave than ever. It was the talk of the clubs and afternoon teas that he had followed her dur-

ing the summer and was desperately in love,
while she was only amusing herself; that she had
rejected him three times, and yet he would not
accept his conge.

Now almost all of their set had gone to the
same place during the hot season, and many other
men had flocked around Miss Kemball without
exciting comment. Miss Kemball, herself, never
spoke of Carl, but Ernai seldom talked of any
of her admirers. The truth was Anson felt her
to be incapable of loving, and patiently served her
and bided his time. He never spoke of love—
indeed, never looked it, and as for proposing
marriage to her, that was still out of the question.
They talked of everything under the sun, and anything beyond, but love was unmentioned. The
sneaking little God sat between them, nevertheless.

Briggs, growing desperate and dauntless, laid
his heart and fortune at her feet, metaphorically
speaking, and was firmly, but gently, refused.
Carl dared not. With him it was happiness to
be allowed to see her often; he could not covet
the possession of her love. It was a bitter contentment.

About this time it went the rounds that Anson
was losing money. He borrowed a great deal
without immediately repaying. People whispered that he was playing too high. He sold his
yacht later on, and the excitement culminated in
a climax when his father declared himself respon-
sible for none of Carl's debts or blunders. Carl
left the paternal mansion, and took elegant rooms
whose rent was not always paid up to time. His
clothes were as tasteful as ever, with the tailor
continually dunning him. He grew pale and
rather thinner than his slender height approved
of, but his beautiful eyes remained still beautiful.
Briggs argued—pleaded to no effect but a storm
of words. He had never before seen Anson lose
his temper, and they had gone all through college
together. Carl, himself, was wretched to the last
degree, and most unsociable. He had not seen
Ernai for three weeks after leaving his father's
house, when, one day she passed him on the street,
and telling the coachman to stop, beckoned Carl
to her carriage.

"Get in with me." She half asked it, half com-
manded.

"Thank you, no. My destination is but three blocks away."

"I will carry you to it, then," she said firmly.

"I will not go with you." He looked at the color making her face pink, and into the surprised brown eyes—those lovely eyes that had first taken his admiration.

"You must drive two squares with me, nevertheless." She opened the door. "Get in," she said, and he obeyed.

"I have heard of your distress," she began, quickly, "for a long time. I sympathize with you, and I wish to see you. Did you think I should deny you my further friendliness because you had lost your fortune? You know I do not. I am your true friend in spite of it. Even despite the fact that I heard you had played it away. That is nonsense. You did not do that, did you?"

What hope there was in the beautiful eyes. He looked at them for long before he answered— till the pink in her checks grew bright.

"Answer me!" she cried, softly.

"Every cent I have lost, has been lost honestly."

"Do you mean by that, you have not lost this money by—gambling?"

"I do," he said—almost sadly, she thought.

"I will trust you," she said.

He bent over her gloved hand, and would have kissed it, but she snatched it from him, just as his reverent lips were thinking to touch it. Her eyes glowed—with anger?

"Ah! Don't be silly," she said. But her voice was not angry. "I will be at home to-morrow evening. Can you call?"

"I will," he said with gentle but meaning emphasis.

"I shall—I will see no one but you. Here is your place." And she dismissed him.

And he? Alas, poor fellow, he did not know what to think; whether she meant to encourage him, or whether her heart (which he knew to be tender), sympathized with him, as he was in trouble. Notwithstanding his perplexity, he was very, very happy, and resolving to let Fate carry him, he gave himself up to thoughts of her remembered face as she looked in the carriage—at one time really more beautiful than he had ever seen it before.

The next night he went to her, cast down to the depths of woe. He resolved to tell her that he loved her—and then Fate should decide the rest.

He passed into the drawing room, and from that to the music room, from whence came the sound of the piano.

He found her alone, a faint flush on her checks, a starry light in the eyes that mocked him.

She was playing softly, and only noticed his entrance with a half smile and a bow. How changeable she was! At one time so cordial, at another so cold! To-night her mood was either —or neither. His heart trembled at the sight and sound; never after can he hear the strain of music that she played but it takes him back to that moment. He can see the dainty room, lit only by the huge, rose-colored piano-lamp; her head half in light, half shadow, inclined a trifle toward the instrument, her lips slightly apart, a smile in the shadowy eyes as she played the soft melody.

He felt his fate coming; he could not resist, though he was not sure that it would be a kind one. He bent down and toward her, and looked into her face.

"Look at me," he whispered.

"No," she whispered back, while a deeper shade flushed her check.

"Don't you know I love you?" he breathed,

4

taking one hand off the keys. She still played on with the other.

"Yes, I know it," she smiled.

"How do you know it?"

"I see it in your eyes."

"Let me see it in yours, Love," he pleaded, bending closer.

For an instant she paused—then raised her lids and looked into his eyes, passionate and deep love in the wonderful, clear-brown glance, till, drunk with its richness he sank on his knees, clasped her close, and drew her lips to his in one long, betrothal kiss.

"What do you think of Anson's trick?" asked Briggs of Trent, a week after. "Pretty clever, eh? You see he'd got some idea that he did not want to be married for his money, and he played the beggar to see if Miss Kemball were worthy. Gad! He might have saved himself the trouble and kept his yacht,—though he will have a new one for the wedding tour—she was his for the asking. Why, man, when he told her he'd been living a lie, she laughed in perfect delight at the notion! Well"— with a tremendous sigh—"He's a good fellow—a fine fellow, and she—well, every one knows what I think of Miss Kemball."

AFTER THE STORM.

Monday evening the sun went down into a golden nest smiling at the pearl shell of a sky; at the placid ocean with ribbons of green against the horizon. Tuesday morning when Brother Felix awoke he found that the sun had not returned. The brown sea curled white lips up at a grey, wild sky. Out in the harbor the oyster smacks were beginning to rock sailless masts to and fro. Brother Felix thought we should have rain; but the coast had been dry for several weeks and the rain would lay the fine, white dust that blew from the shell road.

By four o'clock the wind was a gale. Brother Felix took his book and walked into the convent garden. With one white hand behind him he paced up and down the alley before the Academy. The walk was of white powdered shells, beaten hard, and not very wide. On either side of it was a low green hedge of box, out of which grew a line of cedar trees. The Brother had labored in

the school-room all day and the crisp wind was a
grateful medicine to his lungs.   But the sky being
like a closed blind, the shade of the cedar alley
was too dense for comfortable reading.

Opening the gate, he crossed the narrow street
of the creole town and passed inside the tiny
park which lay between the road and the sea.
The gale blew his cassock about him, and the
salt air struck damp on his face as he walked out
on the frail, narrow pier which trembled in the
clutch of the sea.   Brother Felix loved best to
see his friend, the ocean, thus.   Grey, grey as his
future life, the sky; brown, brown the waves like
the earth which must some day accommodate his
plain coffin.   The wind, too, made such glorious
sighs,—such a long, continuous moan,—that it
saved him the trouble of those silent complaints.
And yet, Brother Felix had seen but thirty years
of life.   His muscular frame would perhaps sweat
in the heat and chill in the cold of many changing
seasons to come.   He struck one hand into the
other and faced about when he reached the end.

The little town,—dear haven of his life,—lay
before him, the greater part of it in plain sight,
stretched like a chain around the wide bay.

Green magnolia trees, spreading live oaks and
sweet gums with mournful grey moss trailing like
tears from their benign branches; blooming
oleanders nodding above white fences like blushes
threatening the face of a maiden; the tops of
verdant pine trees, ambitious to kiss Heaven's
zenith;—he saw, all tossed by the blowing.
There lay the pink college with its rows of arched
white galleries and dormer windows in the roof.
The cottages gleaming like white flowers amidst
the verdure; in front of each a little park with its
summer house, a pier and a bathing shed; the
many colored boats, the quaint, low shops; people
and horses passing to and fro; the gulls flying—
he observed each detail, losing not the slightest
bit of color or movement.

And, was it not strange? What he thought
was: how he wished that Renee could see the
picture!

The wind, for a moment, was silenced by the
cry of anguish that broke from his lips. It had
been so long—Oh God, so long since he had
thought of her! Why had the old habit thrust
itself back upon his heart! He could see her
again,—as plainly as though she came tripping

down the pier toward him,—in a white dress, yes,
in a white dress, and a great hat with auburn
hair against it; and under it gleamed the most
beautiful red-brown eyes that ever harbored
devil's lights to entangle the blindness of man's
love. He had adored her eyes and her hair, her
milk-white skin, and the tiny freckles that lay like
the pricks of a golden pin on her apple-blossom
colored cheek. But best of all he had loved her
own self.

Her plump prettiness was as nothing com-
pared to the witchery of her changing moods.
Her laughter, her smiles were entrancing; her
saucy words, her teasing wit made him desperately wild with warmth of love; but her other self
—that soulful girl with inquiring mind and grand,
noble thoughts—was a being whom he worshipped with respect as one venerates a saint.

Brother Felix crossed himself, nevertheless,
as if she had been the Devil's own dam. Although it was long since he had gazed into those
expressive eyes he could not shake off the fascination of their remembered beauty. If he
prayed into the sky for assistance, out of the grey
cloud they beamed at him full of pity; if he bowed

his head to efface the vision, they laughed up at him in brown mockery. When he looked straight before him he saw the hopeless gaze they had worn when last—when last he really saw them.

He sat him down upon the pier and gave himself up to the memory of it all.

One day when just of age, he had walked up St. Charles Avenue in an idle hour. As he passed a beautiful garden he glanced in and saw, standing under a huge palm tree, a lovely young girl. She was arranging some flowers she had just gathered and quite intent upon her task. She had her back to the street, and as the young man possessed a gentlemanly tread he made no noise. However, he looked steadily at the back of her pretty head, and suddenly she faced about as though some one had called her name.

For one instant they had stood gazing into each other's eyes, and then she made her way across the grass, into the house, without so much as giving him another glance.

And he—what of him? Like one awakened from a dream and not quite sure of earth's reality, he kept repeating to himself: "It is she whom I would like to marry!"

He was proud of the fact that he had compelled her to turn and look at him, and as he was on his way to dine with a friend he quickened pace and hummed a college tune.

Having just been graduated he felt that the world lay before his feet. He could make or mar his life, and he hoped to mold it not only a brilliant but a happy one.

The family of his young host received him cordially, and, after a gay repast, the two young men agreed to make some calls. His friend, Eugene led the way, and—before he realized what had occurred—he found himself in the house of the beautiful garden face to face with her whom he believed his fate.

She was a vision of loveliness in her white dress, and her eyes looked into his with the half frightened gaze of a fawn as she saw his face. Laughingly she told him she remembered having seen him that afternoon, and, like a stage lover, he could have thrown himself at her feet at once.

They remained out upon the wide gallery to be cool, and the young men made but one call that evening. The inevitable Mamma was present, but Eugene had the pleasure of conversing with her.

Through the quiet air the plaintive maternal conversation wandered to Renee and her new found friend, and to him even the mother's voice was disagreeable. The mother herself he disliked upon sight.

Two days later he was again loitering up St. Charles Avenue. It had perhaps been his intention to go to see Eugene. But in a certain garden a charming little maid sat reading a book, and she gave him a friendly nod accompanied by a smile. He had gone inside and spent an hour without heeding that it was dinner time. When her dinner was announced he excused himself and hastened home.

At the end of three weeks, having seen her constantly, he began to feel nervous if a day passed when he could not speak to her. At the expiration of that time something occurred which opened his eyes to a close communication of their spirits. He had found a position, and, leaning over his desk, her face intervened between his eyes and the ledger. He wished he could see her; he wished she would be down town at the noon hour! He had thought it so persistently that when he seized his hat at mid-day, he was sure she

would be upon Canal Street.   He had but turned
the corner when they met.

"Oh!" she laughed, "The funniest thing!   I was
sitting at home mending a rent in a gown.   We
have no telephone in the house, and yet, as plain
as day, I received a message without a messenger.
It said: 'Some one wants to see you down on
Canal Street.'   I tried to resist it.   I have nothing
to buy,—but here I am.   Who can it be do you
suppose that would like so much to see me?"

"Renee," he quietly said, "It was I, wishing for
a sight of you with all my heart, and I have found
you and discovered another thing.   Some day I
shall tell you what."

He was sure now that she loved him.   But
she was such a natural coquette that for more
than a week he could not speak of it.   He saw
her often,—they hardly needed to express a meeting place.   The communion between their souls
was a strong telepathy.   He could almost feel her
moods when they were apart; if they were together there was no barrier to the understanding
between them, so perfect was their love.

When he told her at last, they were in the garden, in the lateral shade of a palm which rose like

a huge mound of feathery banners in the middle
of the yard and formed a screen toward the house.
Why should they, these two, grow serious over
a bit of a poem? Why should it cause them to
think of life with its successes and failures; its
ambitions and heartaches? What sudden sorrow
seared their hearts? Forebodings of evil? She
ceased for the moment to be coquette. She
turned her lovely eyes toward him while she spoke
earnestly of existence being a holy thing, not to
be trifled with. One must make the most of
it. One must not throw one's self into idleness
and disuse, even with money. She smiled di-
vinely when she told him she was glad he had
gone to work. Satan could not then find mischief
for his hands, and he would grow on into good
and noble life.

"Yes," he said, "under certain conditions I
can. Deprived of those circumstances, God
alone knows what will become of me. My life
will only be perfection with you as its dear guide.
Denied that I shall not care for its result. It may
drift as it will. Renee, I love you, I love you!
Give yourself to me and lead me into better paths
than I can find alone!"

She sat looking at him with hands clasped on her knees.

"Ah," she softly said, "You have long ago taken from me any power to dictate. From the moment I first turned and looked into your eyes, I felt that I belonged to you."

It was very trying, it was cruel, there in the sight of chance passers by he could not clasp her in his eager arms. Such emotion, too, comes but once. He hid his face in his hands and felt the sweetness of her words and her look pass over him like a wave of perfume.

That was the happiest moment of his life.

"Renee," he spoke at last, "May I go to your father about it very soon?"

"No," she said quickly, "It is such fun to have our little secret to ourselves for a while. Let us tell no one just yet."

It was the most delightful summer. If he had loved her from the first, it had been but a vague romance. Now, when he knew that she was all his very own he worshipped her with a mad fervor only tempered by the influence which her exceedingly pure spirit held over them both. In the moonlight of the garden, at times, she

seemed to him some fair, white-souled saint from
a higher world. And then she loved him so, she
loved him so,—she made such an adorable sweet-
heart.

The autumn came and Renee said he might
speak to her father. That in itself was not so
difficult for they were on good terms. The older
man had always been kind and genial, and made
his daughter's friend feel welcome in her home.
So it was without a misgiving that the young man
went to him and spake reverently of their mutual
love. It was received by a narrow mind.

"My friend," said Renee's father sadly, "it gives
me the greatest pain to hear this. As far as you
personally are concerned, I admire and trust.
You, however, worship God in the Romanist
faith and are more or less under the control of
the Church. I would rather see my child lie
dead than married to a Catholic! Sooner or
later you would endeavor to convert her. Your
children would be baptized in your faith and not
in hers. I am an elder in the Presbyterian
Church. My ancestors were Huguenots; my
child has been strictly reared within the tenets of
our church."

"Her mother has been suspecting something of this sort, but I refused to send Renee away. I am sorry now that I did not take my wife's advice. I refuse my consent to such a union and I am sure her mother will also."

Arguments, protestations, promises were of no avail. He went out of the office feeling stunned and crushed. Meeting Renee by previous appointment, they went to the little church of St. Roch's, where they prayed and wept together. They swore never to marry unless they could marry each other.

That was the last time he saw her alone. The mother was more incensed than the father, and Renee was kept under strict surveillance.

A suddenly planned voyage to Europe was carried out and Renee was taken abroad.

At the expiration of two years, morose, embittered, her lover entered the Brotherhood. Renee had not returned and Brother Felix had never heard of her since he left New Orleans.

Resolutely, day by day, he had put her out of his thoughts until now as she persisted in standing before his memory, he felt that something unusual had happened. Something beyond his

power to control caused him to dream thus of
her. Where was she? Was she alive? Did she
still think of him? Had she become the wife of
another, or was she still faithful as she promised
to be? Sad and sick at heart, with bowed head,
he arose and walked back above the heaving
water.

The wind was growing cold to him, and, having
reached the shore end of the pier, he crossed
once more the grass-plot with its stiff row of
palms, over the shell road and into the Academy
yard, just as the church clock chimed five.

The pretty church of Our Lady of the Gulf
lay between two convents. One was a school
for girls kept by gentle Sisters; the other was the
Academy for boys, in which Brother Felix
taught. The Sisters wore bonnets and shoulder
capes of white, spotless linen and gowns of black
serge. The Brother's costume was all of black;
a cassock, a girdle, and at the back a heavy pleat
which swayed loose in the wind. Gentle lives
they led in that little town, adored by their young
charges, beloved by the creole fisher-folk and
citizens. For they did much good to the poor
and God rewarded them by giving them the

bountiful love of the people. One could see
in what respect they were held as they passed
through the street. If a Sister went out she was
accompanied by another Sister, or a little girl.
The women stopped her and chattered in French,
perhaps about the progress of the children; the
negroes greeted her with humble reverence in
their patois; the little girls clustered around
in more familiar admiration. The Brothers
went about independently, and, perchance, because they were men, in spite of being Brothers,
there was not the meekness of bearing in their
manner as in that of the Sisters.

Twilight came down gently, softly, adding
another neutral shade to the landscape. Night
and Storm were coming together, hand in hand.

There was a pair of anxious eyes at the extreme
end of the village that night. It is difficult for
one to sleep in a strange bed, in an alien town,
but on this occasion it was more of a task than
ever. The whole world was awake and astir as
though its nerves were throbbing and sentient
like those of the young woman who heard the
wind howling amongst the crevices. As the
darkness grew deeper and nothing remained of

outdoors but the sound of waves and trees, she stirred uneasily in her chair, then slowly turned to a table by her side and rang a silver bell.

The sound of light feet upon the gallery, the doors gently opened and shut in quick succession preceded a softly modulated voice asking what she wanted.

"Please, Miss Bent, tell Mat'ile to bring the lamp, and to come build me a fire."

The door closed softly, the dainty step retreated. A few moments later the outer doors slammed, the shuffling scrape of Mathile's walk could be heard, and she entered with difficulty. First she set down her bucket of wood and opened a door, holding in one hand the lamp which shone upon her dusky face. Then she moved the bucket inside and afterwards closed the portal. Having reached the room, she put the lamp upon a table and began her task of building the fire.

"We gwine hev a bad night, Momzelle," she said, lighting a match. "Ah theenk it will stohm."

"Oh, Mat'ile!"

"Yis, Momzelle, Ah'm jis' sho' it will. Mat'ile

don't mek no mistek about de wedda." She held a small stick over the flame of her match until it ignited. Then she placed that in the deep, square fireplace and piled pine knots upon it. Finally, the logs were laid upon the blaze and a banner of light streamed into the black mouth of the chimney.

"Mathile," said the slow voice of Mademoiselle de Montluzin, "you know how to build a fire."

She spoke with such evident effort, so weakly, that one understood why she did not say much. The lamp, lighting up the pillowed chair wherein she sat, proclaimed her an invalid. She was, alas, no convalescent. Those large, bright eyes, those pale, sunken cheeks with the little pink spot on the check bones; one could read their story at a glance. Mathile, big, fat, old Mathile, with her gaudy bandana about her head and huge rings of gold in her ears, stood and gazed at her mistress with fascinated agony in her heart. She had watched Mlle. de Montluzin thus for three years. Her mission was to make her young mistress cheerful, however, so she talked a great deal.

"It teks de onnerstannin'," said Mathile, apro-

pos of the fire. "W'en a body ain' got no onnerstannin', dey mek a lee'le ting be heap o' wuk.
W'en dey's got de onnerstannin', dey mek a gret
big wuk on'y a lee'le ting."

Mademoiselle smiled at this philosophy.

"Momzelle Bent, now she got de onnerstannin',
uh? She know jis' w'at to do at de right time.
En de tings she mek yo' to eat, she fix jis' so,
uh? W'at dat yo' call 'er?"

"A trained nurse."

Mathile gave a frank stare of appreciation at
this, but she did not attempt to repeat it. Nodding her head, she said:

"Well, I nu's yo' fus'."

Mademoiselle laughed.

"Miss Bent is a sick nurse," she said.

"I nu's yo' w'en yo' lec'le chile; w'en yo' fus'
bohn. How long 'go wuz dat, Momzelle?"

"Twenty-seven years, Mathile."

"Twent'-se'm yeah! Oh! Cahn't be dat long."

"Yes; I was twenty-three, you know, when
mother died."

"En 'ow ole w'en M'sieu Hubert wan'd yo to
mahy 'im?"

"Hush, Mathile, do not speak of that. It is

best that I didn't marry him, nor any one else. You see what I have come to."

"Oh, but, chile, da wan't none o' um lak M'sieu' Hubert. An' ef on'y Mom Montluzin 'ad 'a' let yo' mahy 'im, yo' wouldn't 'a' woyied yo'se'f sick. No, Momzelle."

At this juncture, Miss Bent came into the room, bearing a tray, and the invalid prepared to eat supper. Mathile shuffled out with empty bucket, allowing the wind to slam the doors behind her as she went.

Miss Bent attended to the wants of her charge, mended the fire, made ready for the night, and then sat down for a chat. She was a cheery little body, soft-eyed and pink-cheeked, not a quarter of a century old and with a most undeniable talent for nursing. Her ways were not only scientific, but picturesque as well, and Mlle. de Montluzin admired to gaze at her. She wore a grey gown, white cap, kerchief and apron.

"I hope the storm will not be bad," she began. "It will not frighten you, will it?"

"No," said the invalid. "Death would be as welcome now as at any time. I am only thinking of you."

Miss Bent laughed.

"Do not think of me," she cried. "There is no one left to mourn my taking off. Besides, I have faced death too often to fear it."

"I am sorry my father and brother could not have come over with us."

"Never mind," said Miss Bent, cheerfully, "they will be here Saturday. Certainly they could have done no better in the selection of a cottage than did old Mathile. But, then, she has been with your family so long, I dare say she understands the individual tastes of each member."

"She drives a bargain well, too," said the slow voice of the sick woman. The nurse did not permit her patient to talk much. She chatted freely, herself, amusing Mademoiselle by little anecdotes and personal experiences, brightening the dull moments.

Mlle. de Montluzin was finally tucked in bed and the nurse went to her own rest in an adjoining room. Neither of the women could find much sleep. The wind howled a minor song, and the cottage seemed to brace itself against the attacks of its breezy adversary. Like all far Southern cottages, it was built upon piles or pil-

lars, several feet off the ground, having no cellar
or basement. As it was a two-story house with
deeply gabled roof, the rain made very little noise
to one on the lower floor, but in the depth of the
night Miss Bent suddenly sat up in bed.

She had heard the unmistakable sound of lap-
ping, rushing water underneath.

Brother Felix was aroused next morning before the proper time. Like the hearty athlete he
was, he had slept peacefully through the wildest
storm the coast had known for many years. At
the summons he arose and went to his window.
The sky was clear, but waves mountains high,
were still rolling in. Before his sight went down
a pier and a bath house as though built of cards.
The Academy pier was already gone—so was the
next—and the next! Two of the little shops on
the shore—the grand old trees uprooted—boats
thrown high on the embankment; boats floating
keel uppermost in the water! Brother Felix
opened his window and gazed up the beach.
The piers were all gone! Only skeleton posts
remained. The breakwater was down and part

of the shell road had caved in. Brother Felix
buried his face in his hands.

When he reached the outer world, he found,
as he had surmised, that a tidal wave had swept up
to the town. Then began the work of assistance.
Many boats in the harbor overturned meant
grievous loss of life there. He helped to recover
some of the bodies. Tangled hair, matted with
tangled seaweed; driftwood for a pillow; white
sand for a bed. Yet, they had died peacefully
enough; drowning is an easy death. This was
his one crumb of comfort for the wild-mouthed
widows and mothers. Only once did his heart
fail him—when pretty Elise threw herself upon
the body of him she was so soon to have wedded.
Brother Felix fled.

There would be one more nun to serve the
Church of Our Lady of the Gulf.

It would shock you to tell the dreadful tales he
heard, the sights that met his eyes. In the afternoon, a young negro lad came to him, telling of
a case needing assistance.

"Da's a sick leddy en' anodda leddy, en' a culled
ooman out da at de house on de p'int. Ah drobe
um out da mase'f w'en dee cum ova' on de cahs,

en' Ah ben out da dis mawnin', en' de house mos' tu'n ova', en' de watah hit all up 'roun de house."

Brother Felix was wild with pity. The boats had all washed away! What was to be done? Finally, the boy told of one that was stowed under cover, and with great difficulty they procured that.

The sun was pacing down his western halls when they started. It was about three o'clock. The sea had worn itself out, beating calmer with every stroke of the waves, until it lay like a giant opal, heaving in long stretches of color, almost motionless. The cloudless sky placed no obstruction in the path of the great shining sun. Brother Felix and the boy bent to the oars and went along the stricken coast in mournful silence. The house loomed in sight at last, lying very much tilted indeed. The tidal wave had lifted it off its piles. As they drew nearer, they observed a woman waving a white cloth from one of the windows. The cottage on the point had been cut off as though it were an island. The swollen waters were not yet subsided. Brother Felix brought the boat as close as possible, then tramped over the sopping sands to the entrance, climbing up by the remains of broken timbers.

The woman had opened the door for him, and stood waiting.

"God bless you for coming," said Miss Bent, "I have in my care a lady who is dying of pulmonary consumption, and the shock she received last night has sapped all of her nervous strength. Can we possibly get her to the hotel?"

"Let us hope so," responded the Brother.

"I shall prepare her to see you," said the nurse. She quickly ran upstairs. For thither, with old Mathile's help, she had carefully assisted her patient. Presently she returned and bade their visitor follow her.

Brother Felix entered the presence of Mlle. de Montluzin with bared head. Miss Bent, having announced his mission, went to make ready for their departure—to search for dry blankets and pillows to place in the boat.

"Madame," said Brother Felix, as he bowed, "I am come with a boat to assist you back to the village."

He was standing in the full light and could see only part of her face because of the deep shadows cast upon it. But he could see enough to observe sadly sunken cheeks, a wasted figure against the pillows. She did not ask him to be seated. She had not spoken. Brother Felix began to feel nervous.

"The sea is no longer rough," he said, gently. "We can row you to the hotel quite easily. It is calm."

There was another silence, and then, in the dragging, painful fashion of her speech, she said:

"Stand here—in front—by the window—and look at me. Do you not know me, Hubert?"

He had crossed the room at her first command. He had paled to the lips. Terror took possession of his face. In one instant it seemed to age and wither. He gazed into her enlarged brown eyes, her face so changed, and then he blotted out the vision with his hands, murmuring:

"Not Renee; not my Renee! Oh!"

"Come to me, Hubert," she said, holding out one shrunken hand. The hectic spot on her cheek burned bright; her eyes glowed with a new light and softness. "Kneel down here by my chair. That is right. Let me place my hand on your head. Nay, why do you weep? Is it the change you behold in me? I have changed inwardly, too. The sea is no longer rough in my heart. It is calm. The storm, it is true, destroyed the fibers of my being, but I am content. You, too, are at peace. It is well. And yet—there is one thing I lack to make me happy, quite, quite happy. Tell me, do you still love me—in spite of it all? I have always loved you as I promised I should. They could part our bodies, but my heart, my spirit, was always with you, Hubert."

He bent over her hands clasped in his and kissed them. The tears rained down his cheeks as he told her of his devotion. He broke his vows, in thought, there on his knees to Renee. Warm, passionate kisses upon her hands seemed a balm to that tired soul. She sat up straight.

"Some other day—some other time—some other life," she said, smiling, nodding. "We shall love each other again, Hubert."

She fell back against the pillows. Renee de Montluzin had become but a memory.

Brother Felix labored for the stricken townspeople. He had always been grave, quiet, but now a gentleness pervaded his actions, a sympathy drew his fellow-creatures to him which was unlike any trait they had observed before. And when the worst distress was over, it was Brother Felix whom most frequently they extolled. Still stands the little church of Our Lady of the Gulf. The Academy yard is green, the hedge is kept closely trimmed; the bordered walk is white and firm. Up and down the sheltered alley passes Brother Felix in his black cassock. Not so strong his figure, not so black his soft hair. But he smiles as he walks; his hands clasp together. He raises his head and looks upward, as he whispers:

"Some other day—some other time—some other life."

THE LADY OF THE GULF.

Hot the sunshine poured to earth from the molten crucible of the sun, but a cooling breeze blew from the deep blue gulf like a breath of benediction. Against the cerulean heavens the verdure of the tree tops looked like emeralds in a turquoise setting. A low, moaning wind blowing through the eolian harp of the pines, at the same time pilfered their fragrance. Incense and music it brought to Brother Felix as he rested in the yard of the convent, under the shade of a glossy magnolia tree.

While he sat thus reading his favorite paper in the holiday time, the young priest of the village came from the Academy door and walked toward the magnolia, pausing on his way across the grass to look at the marble sundial. He and Brother Felix had become great friends. They had seen each other once before on this bright morning.

"Well, how does he carry himself?" asked Brother Felix.

6

"Poorly," answered Father Renaud, "very poorly, indeed. I believe," he continued, shaking his head, "that the good old Father will soon be enjoying the rest he has earned."

"Indeed," said the Brother sadly, "He was a good shepherd to this little flock. I suppose you have found since you came to take his place, that the villagers love him as a real father."

"Yes, Brother Felix, he and another, whose name I need not mention, seem to have wound themselves about the hearts of the people. I am afraid that even more than the memory of Father Bourgeois, I shall have to contend against the presence of Brother Felix."

"Nonsense!" said Felix, smiling and flushing, "you flatter me. Besides, all the affection I have obtained has been through long and earnest labor. You seem to have captured them at once with that wonderful quality known as personal magnetism."

"My life!" softly laughed the young priest. "What a mutual admiration society we are!"

His laugh was as frank and open as his face, and Brother Felix smiled broadly in response, showing fine, white teeth.

They chatted upon all subjects freely, enjoying

that stimulus to conversation which comes when two people are aware that they like each other upon short acquaintance. Then, too, they neither one were very old, the priest being the younger.

He was a man twenty-eight years old, fully six feet tall, possessing a slender, noble figure, with a small head of admirable contour. His hair had an auburn shade, and a decided wave in it; his brown eyes were soft and dark, their lashes as long as a girl's, and very black. His complexion was clear; the features were molded upon a firm but delicate cast, the whole countenance bespeaking purity and candor. Brother Felix could not account for the warmth he felt toward Father Renaud. It was beyond admiration for his eloquence; it was much more than fascination. He decided that it was because their hearts were tuned in the same key.

Brother Felix, having few joys and fewer loves, accepted it as a consolation and rejoiced.

Father Renaud had been sent to relieve Father Bourgeois in his failing old age. Now the old Father was really dying; having received his last sacrament, he had lost consciousness, and it remained but to wait for the end.

"I have been here for nine weeks to-day," said the young priest. Once more looking at the sun-dial, he remarked: "I must go to the church now to hear confessions. By the way, I am charmed with the name of the church. 'Our Lady of the Gulf.' It is so appropriate."

"Yes," said Brother Felix, "it pleases the fisher-men. They always speak of it with individual regard."

"Au revoir," said the priest.

"Good day," replied the Brother, and sat watch-ing the handsome figure of Philippe Renaud go across the grass, observing that the black cassock enhanced its grace. Alas, he thought, what a pity the priesthood could not marry! Celibacy was only meant for the old, the disappointed, the disconsolate—not for a care-free youth like that! With a sigh he turned back to his reading.

Father Renaud wended his way to the church. It lay not far from the Academy, a gray stone structure, with the slender spire pointing above a gold marked clock as if to say: "Thy time on earth is short; prepare for heaven." There were sev-eral people in the church, scattered about, kneeling, gazing abstractedly into their own souls, as they moved their lips in prayer.

The little church was proud of its three highly decorated altars. There were some excellent paintings that had been done in Paris. The holy water font was a huge shell lying on a pedestal. There was one side altar to St. Joseph. It was draped in white and gold; fragrant flowers stood in its vases; the ornaments were of good design and the tapers were fresh. Over the altar was a beautiful picture with several figures in it. That representing the Christ was a manlier type than such faces usually are. The one of the Virgin had a most life-like expression. It quite haunted Father Renaud for a fortnight after he arrived, until one day he spoke of it to Brother Felix.

"It is good," smiled the Brother. "The reason it strikes you so forcibly is that you have seen the face it was painted from. The picture was injured by a ladder which fell against it when a workman was repairing the window. It remained with the face of the Madonna badly scarred until about six months ago. A young artist then strayed into the village, and it happened that he knew Father Bourgeois. As he had taken several medals in Paris, the Father looked upon him in the light of a divine messenger and gave him an order to replace the head.

"The young painter asked me whether there were any pretty nuns over at the convent. I told him he might see them on the street at any time. To me they are all beautiful from their consecration."

"In that," commented Father Renaud, "they all resemble the Madonna."

"Is it not so?" said Brother Felix. "The artist smiled at my remark and answered that to him a saint-like countenance seemed more holy when it was beautiful. In the congregation on Sunday he spied the face of young Sister Cecilia. At once he desired to use her for a model for Our Lady. The sittings were permitted by Mother Elizabeth, and she herself accompanied Sister Cecilia to pose."

The young priest was silent for a moment, studying the face above the altar. At length he remarked:

"Yes, I think that must be it. If I remember correctly she has charge of the younger children."

"That is Sister Cecilia," responded his friend.

To say the least, that one face was the best of the group. Likely enough the later life of the Holy Mother was not an altogether peaceful, reposeful one, and in this face was something that coincided with such a theory. It lacked the calm, china-doll expression of ordinary Madonnas. There was longing, wonder, questioning. Was it also this, perhaps, that made one remember it?

Upon the altar under the picture were many little slabs of marble engraved and bearing the gilded legends: "Merci," or "Thanks," sometimes with the date, also. In a near corner were discarded crutches and canes.

The other side altar was similar. The confession box which Father Renaud occupied, was half way down a side aisle.

Father Renaud was not fond of hearing confessions. Sometimes they made him secretly angry; sometimes they made him sad. It was one of his tasks which he performed from a strict sense of duty. Nothing of note occurred this warm afternoon until the end of the time usually given to the audience. The church was empty once more and he was preparing to leave, when the door opened and two sisters came silently down the aisle.

Father Renaud waited until they reached him. The foremost sister was an elderly woman, round and fat, with steel spectacles prominent beneath her white linen bonnet. Following Mother Elizabeth came she whose title Father Renaud had heard from Brother Felix seven weeks before. It was Sister Cecilia.

Being tall, she could look over the Mother Superior's head. Her eyes, as she walked up the dark aisle were fixed intently upon the priest. Gray eyes they were, a pure grey like the sky which hangs above a snowy landscape. But they had another quality in unison with the clouds— they could deepen and darken, and moist drops fell from them, too. She had almost too much color. When she smiled she had deep dimples. Her cheeks were rather plump but she had a small, round chin. The face, with its glow and mobility of expression, was not the serene countenance of a nun. Her slender figure, erect carriage, graceful movement, had no place clad in black serge. She was too much the goddess in form to be the disciple in spirit.

Father Renaud, watching her figure sway up the dark aisle, likened it to a wind-blown poppy. He knew that beneath that snowy cape fluttered a heart as wild and warm as the crimson field flower. He was her confessor. For two months in the discharge of his duty he had learned of the restless, life-loving character, and, knowing of her what he did, he said to himself:

" I wonder what is coming now?"

Mother Elizabeth plumped her rotund body down into a pew. Sister Cecilia remained standing in the aisle motionless, while Mother Elizabeth spoke.

" I have brought her here to you again. This time talk to her yourself. You are her spiritual adviser; perhaps she will tell you why she wants to go away from this place."

"To go away?" calmly echoed Father Renaud.

He looked into the grey eyes of Sister Cecilia. Then he looked down upon the stone pavement.

"Tell me the trouble, Mother."

" I cannot. She is restless and unhappy. Usually I can give advice to those under my charge without assistance. But in this case my kindest efforts are of no avail. She meekly carries out the penance inflicted; she obeys my rules; she is an excellent teacher to the little ones, and yet— she is forever dissatisfied. She renders all St. Mary's unhappy. Then when I demand to know what is the reason, she only begs me to let her go away. She has asked me to transfer her."

"Reverend Mother," said the priest quietly, "withdraw a bit and I will talk to her."

The Superioress accordingly went to the back of the church. Father Renaud entered the confessional, and Sister Cecilia knelt in the place of penitents.

Mother Elizabeth also knelt and prayed. Then she ceased and opened her eyes and looked through the length of the church at the altar dedicated to St. Joseph. Over it was the picture for which had posed the exquisite face of Sister Cecilia. Suddenly there came a flash of memory, recalling the young artist who painted it. How he had gazed at his model! The Mother Superior began to speculate on probabilities.

Sister Cecilia had been in the order but a year. Why she had joined the sisterhood, no one could tell. Her mother, weeping, had said it was done in a moment of religious enthusiasm. Her best friend, a girl of expressed opinions, said stoutly:

"Nonsense! She did it to find out what it was like. She had tired of society in three years; she had never found the consolation of falling in love, so she took the vows to get away from it."

That was not a fair estimate in its entirety, but it was a near approach to the truth. Marie said Suzanne Benoit had found life a bore without love. The men she met wearied her, everything wearied her in the artificial glare of society. She desired to be an artist, but her mother was violently opposed to anything so bohemian and professional. The mother was a woman of superficial character, a bundle of overwrought nerves, and selfish to the core. Susanne might have taken the vows to escape from her tyranny.

Nevertheless, once received into the sisterhood she regretted her course. Mother Elizabeth, toward whom she was as reticent as she dared be, would have enjoyed keen surprise to hear her as she poured out her grief to the good Father Renaud.

"Ever since I first saw you standing there at the altar," said Sister Cecilia, "I felt that you would help me. Perhaps I am mistaken. The whole truth is this:

"Last winter a young man painted the Madonna over the St. Joseph shrine from me. Watching him handle the brushes, knowing of the success he had achieved—nay even the very smell of the oil made me restless. I want to get away. I do not care for the world, Father, I could do without it beautifully—society, I mean. But oh, I so long to be an artist! To go to Paris and study! I have often thought that if I could only have married a man who would let me study painting, I would have been happy, though I did not love him. I made such a mistake to come here."

"My child," said the low voice of Father Renaud, "are you sure, quite sure, that it is the painting you long to do, or is it a romantic attachment you have fostered for this young artist—is it a marriage you seek? Nay, listen to me. I wish first to tell you that here in this place where you kneel, time after time I hear the sighs and complaints of people, men and women who are married, but who, upon one side or the other, find that lack of love which renders marriage a hollow mockery. There is only one life that satisfies one fully. It is the spiritual existence."

"But Father," sadly said Sister Cecilia, "I have not found it so, for I am not content! I wish to leave the order."

"You can study painting. You can be a teacher in one of the advanced convent schools. You can send your work outside and you can win a fame amongst your scholars."

"And that would take me away from St. Mary's?" she asked joyfully.

The priest was silent for a moment. When at length he found his speech it was calm and slow.

"You have not yet answered me in regard to this young man. I shall give you a few days to think over what you will say to me—"

"Oh, let me—"

"Nay, do not answer now. You will go in silence and commune with yourself about this matter. You will tell me your thoughts. But not to-day. Next Saturday. You will have learned your heart by that time. You may tell me then all about it."

"But Father, I know my heart now."

"Daughter, I wish you first to think about it."

Tears of vexation sprang to her eyes, but she meekly bowed her head.

The priest dismissed her and she rejoined Mother Elizabeth in a silence that could only end by the solace of weeping.

The good old Father Bourgeois was dead. Such a funeral had never been seen in the village. Barouche after barouche came into the town, each drawn by the lean and tiny pony which abounds on the coast and its islands. These little horses are never even plump, but in spite of their meagre dimensions, they can draw heavy loads, and that, too, with a jaunty indifference. They make one think of the rats which Cinderella's Fairy Godmother changed to horses, one of which must have stopped half way in its growth.

At a funeral it is not seemly to ridicule the cortege, of course, and the natives being accustomed to these little rats of horses, only drove to the ceremony or in the procession with grave faces and sad hearts.

The little church was crowded to suffocation. It was very, very warm; but despite the heat, despite the environment, there was a deep atten-

tion and a sense of the brevity of time as they
listened to Father Renaud's funeral oration.

It was sublime, uplifting; it was an inspiration.
He pointed the way to a better life and made one
long to lead it. His eloquence held them spell-
bound as he showed them what a beautiful example their priest had set them, and when he had
ceased talking there was a hush and pause over
the congregation.

The old priest, glorified, being laid to rest,
Father Renaud remained in the village to fill his
place.

The Thursday after the funeral—not quite a
week since Sister Cecilia came to confession with
Mother Elizabeth—was a bright, clear day. The
landscape lay wreathed in deep summer green.
If one were upon it, one perceived the earth to be
dry and hot. Down in one corner of the horizon,
over the water, a bunch of snow white clouds
were clustered, fluffy nestlings against the breast
of their mother, air. But clouds were not always
a sure sign of rain. One was sometimes led to
believe that they were but a natural adjunct to
the sublime beauty of the scene; part of the stage
setting for sunsets and bright mornings.

Father Renaud was standing at the gate of the Academy talking to several of the Brothers. A small boy ran across the street and came up to the group, panting. Little, flat, moist curls against his brow, red cheeks, dusty bare feet, all betokened haste and heat.

"Please, Brother Felix," he said in gasps, "won't you take us boys somewhere to-day? Sister Cecilia's takin' my little sister's class out on the North Hill, an' they're goin' to have dinner out there an' have a picnic."

There was a general smile on the faces of the men in the group, but no sound escaped except the voice of Brother Felix. Up the street a little procession could be seen, children walking two by two, and a Sister bending over them here and there, the white wings of her cornette gleaming in the sunshine. Father Renaud knew she was smiling and chatting merrily with them as she adjusted their belongings or their positions. She was going with them alone. Well, she would certainly have her hands full!

" Emile," said Brother Felix, "it is too late now. Why did you not come to me yesterday? You could not gather the boys together on such short notice. We can go Saturday. Will that do?"

Emile paused a moment and fingered his torn straw hat.

"Oh, couldn't we please go to-day?"

"I'm afraid not, my little man," replied the good Brother. "We should want an abundance to eat for twenty hungry boys, and it takes time to prepare the games. We will go on Saturday and you may go and tell the boys now if you wish."

"All right," said Emile. He smiled brightly, jammed his battered hat tightly on his curly brown head and bounded away. Brother Felix looked after him with a tender light on his handsome face.

"Would that I were in that little fellow's shoes," he said.

"Why, he's barefooted!" exclaimed Father Renaud. Brother Felix gracefully acknowledged the burst of laughter which ensued, and they stood watching the little girls' procession as it passed out of sight.

Then, hanging on the gate, the quartet resumed their heated discussion. It was concerning the ex-priest who had been mobbed in a northern

7

town because he had married. It was argued at
length amongst them. Brother Felix expressed
his opinion that he was right to have married.
He believed in the marriage of the clergy, for
even our Master had said it is not good for man
to live alone.

"But," said Father Renaud, "Christ chose a
life of celibacy."

"Why?" asked Brother Felix. "Did you ever
reason it out? Did you ever picture to yourself
what the result would have been in modern times?
Think! He came on earth to render all men
equal. He founded a religion which worships
Him as having sprung from God. If Christ had
married, His children would have been worshipped as saints, even in life. His descendants
would be revered as the highest type of human-
kind. It would have created an aristocracy more
despotic than that made by the blue blood of
kings of earth. It would have been a danger
and a menace to the very social and moral laws
He taught. His far-seeing mind perceived that
matrimony was not for Him, although in other
men He sanctioned and blessed it. It is the
only way to live in purity and contentment!"

Brother Felix was riding his hobby. The other men, though ripe for argument, remained silent. There were a thousand unuttered questions on their lips, and a deep wonder filled them that Brother Felix should be living a life with which he was not in sympathy. But since the tragic death of Mlle. de Montluzin, a mysterious romance had been woven about him, and men are such gossips that each of them there knew as much as any one else. Regard for Brother Felix now closed their lips. In the embarrassed pause which followed, Father Renaud said:

"Friends, I must away from this edifying assemblage. I would like to find a letter from my good mother waiting for me at the post-office. May I ask for letters for one or all of you?"

Having received their negatives and their polite thanks, he parted from them and strode down the village street whose dust vibrated in parched thirst unslaked.

He found a letter for him—a letter just like those he received once a week, full of love and affection and pride. But the missive to-day had one paragraph in it which seemed to trouble him. He read it several times, then closed his hand

with a fierce grip over the paper and strode on
in the quivering heat. Away from the convent,
away from the pavements and the town, out
towards the trees and the free country, until he
found himself at the little wooded slope they called
North Hill.

He paused and wondered how he had reached it
so quickly. And yet he did not return. The
shade of the great, moss-hung live oaks was so
cool; the palmettos under his feet looked greener
and fresher; the woods were broad, were inviting.
Being half way up the hill by this time, he gave
his attention to the serious task of climbing, and
—suddenly came with a start of surprise upon
Sister Cecilia, with her embroidery lying idle as
she watched him walk towards her. She sat with
her back against a tree. The children were
scattered about in her sight, and if they wandered
too far, she blew a silver whistle for them to come
within bounds. They were playing little games
and busy with their own affairs.

Father Renaud sat down upon the ground
facing her.

Sister Cecilia's face was by no means too rosy
now, for it was very white. She raised her head

higher with a snake-like, graceful movement, and in an instant had changed from the meek nun to the woman of the world.

"Why did you come here!" she demanded. "Who told you where I was?" She looked at him with dark, angry eyes; her color came surging back.

Father Renaud sat gazing at her with hands clasped about his knees. His black cassock and white collar set off the clear pallor of his cheek. Only the lips were red, and his mouth not at all that of the prelate. His eye lids closed with a momentary expression of weariness, and then opened wide to look full at her.

"I came unawares," he quickly said. "Old habit, I suppose, the old fascination—your never failing power over me. And I have you alone at last. I am going to give you a bit of my mind and you will have to listen."

She leaned against the tree trunk for a moment, scanning his face. Then she sat upright, smiling that roguish, dimpled smile, and raised the silver whistle to her lips.

Father Renaud gave a little gasp.

After all, she did not blow it, but let it fall and took up her embroidery.

"Suzanne," he said sadly, "still the coquette."

"No," she said quite gravely, "I have an object in life now; it is only when one has nothing serious in one's thoughts that one can be a coquette."

"You an object in life—you?"

"Yes, ah, yes! And I shall not tell what it is, even if you are my Father Confessor."

Suddenly she raised her head and looked at him scornfully. "How can you, oh, how can you pretend so!"

"I must," he answered firmly. "It is for your own sake. If they knew—ah! If they knew that you had flouted me and led me on and played with my heart and finally thrown me over! If they knew that the reason for my earnest devotion to the Church was because I could not devote my life to you, they would send you away. But you cannot go away!"

The girl looked at him with half-frightened eyes.

"I am at the head of this parish," he said quietly. Then he softly said: "Ah, Suzanne, what a pity

it is! How young you were—how young to
have controlled two destinies! Do you remember? I recall every phase of it. I know your
very words by heart; but that is merely because
I had a good memory and because it was the
turning-point in my life. Bah! I thought I
had forgotten it. And then Fate led me blindly
to this town. When they showed me the church,
I saw your face as the face of Our Lady of the
Gulf. What a mockery! And yet, no, for through
you, my lady, I had encountered a gulf of trouble.
The next Sunday as I stepped before the congregation, my brain seemed to fairly reel as I looked
upon your living, upturned face."

"You did not know I had taken the vows?"
she asked.

"No. I had never heard from you. I had
tried to blot you out of my life. God knows I
tried to do so conscientiously."

He bent his head until his brow touched his
knees. Then he raised himself.

"However, when we met, I made no sign.
Neither did you. Brother Felix told me the story
of the painting over the altar. You yourself told
me you were restless because of it. Mother Eliz-

abeth has confided her fears that you love that man!"

"Remember," she began, with a twinkle in her eyes, "I am not to tell you of that affair till Saturday!"

"Oh, Suzanne, Suzanne! Don't you understand that that was all sham! Do you not see that I was afraid Mother Elizabeth's sharp ear would catch our words? I was afraid to hear the truth even in my official capacity. I was afraid we would betray ourselves. But here, under God's wide heaven, we are face to face as man and woman! Tell me the truth. I promise you to put aside all my selfish, futile thoughts of you. What right have I to think of you? If you love him tell me so, and I shall help you to escape and to marry him!"

Father Renaud had paused, leaning forward in an agonized intensity.

"Listen, Philippe," she began softly. "Do not go quite so swiftly. Let us begin far back, with ourselves. It is true I did trifle with you wretchedly. I was young, as you say—so young that life had only infinite possibilities and no horizon whatsoever. I adored you, with it all. I quite

expected you to return when I sent you away.
When you did not, I was at first piqued, then
melancholy; then I affected indifference. My in-
timates could not understand why I never fell in
love. The reason was that no one came up to
you where you were mounted on my pedestal.
When I heard you had entered the priesthood,
my heart stood still, aghast.

"'Well,' I said, 'here is nothing left but for
me to enter a convent.'

"But the world is sweet to me, and I could
not bear to think of being shut up, so I chose to
be a teaching Sister. I have tried to be contented.
I submerged myself in my new duties. Then
came that artist to paint the Madonna. I never
saw him alone. I sat patiently, day after day,
while he and Mother Elizabeth talked incessantly
of—what do you think? Of the failing powers
of Father Bourgeois, of the priest who would
probably be called to take his active work—the
brilliant young Philippe Renaud! Now, do you
wonder at the expression on the face of Our
Lady?"

She looked at him with questioning eyes, as

though she was not quite sure she should have told him. She continued:

"The artist went away. I never gave him a tender thought. But every time I went into the church I saw that portrait. I thought not of the artist. Through my head rang his continual praises of your name. And then, you came—

"So you see," she said, nodding her head and blinking tear-filled eyes, " you must help me to go away."

She dropped her face in her hands and silently wept while Philippe plucked at the grass with downcast lids. Quickly drying her tears, she placed the little whistle to her lips and blew three shrill notes. That was the signal for dinner. He helped her prepare the meal. The children were all fond of him and hailed him with delight.

Father Renaud stayed to dinner with them, but after the luncheon, he went down the hill and along the hot, dusty road to the village. As he walked he once more read his mother's letter, and the paragraph which troubled him. It ran thus:

" I am often lonely and restless now in my old age. I could wish at times that your life had been different; that you, my only son, could have married and had children to play about my knees in this big house. Yet you followed my wishes and I must abide by the result. Your father has never ceased to mourn your vocation in life. With you, he says, the race becomes extinct."

He thrust the letter back into his cassock and proceeded on his way. The smile of renunciation illumined his features, and a steadfast purpose beamed in the dark, soft eyes. Once more, he thought of Sister Cecilia; again he saw her preparing lunch with the children clustered around her as she bent over the white cloth on the grass. Again he saw her expressive face as he talked with her apart while the little ones ate unheeding.

Friday morning there was the greatest consternation in the convent. Nuns were running forward to Mother Elizabeth, and the Mother Superior in turn waddled her fat body in haste back to the bare little closet of Sister Cecilia.

Everything was in order, but there was little to disturb.

Hanging up in one corner were the coarse

black serge gown, the white bonnet and cape, the chain and girdle which were wont to softly envelop the form of Sister Cecilia. Poking the folds of the habit, Mother Elizabeth found a note pinned to the fabric. She hastily tore it open and read:

"Reverend Mother Superior: Adieu, adieu, kind, good woman. I know thou wilt not miss my troublesome spirit, and I beg thee not to fret over my mysterious exit. I am gone into the world to seek a broader life, and, please God, to find happiness.

"SISTER CECILIA."

In great dismay, the Superioress set forth to the Academy to consult with Father Renaud.

Alas! At the Academy, also, there was running to and fro and shaking of heads.

Philippe Renaud, the noble young priest of such brilliant promise, had fled from the village.

His black cassock hung upon the hook in his bedroom, and pinned within its folds they found a note.

"Farewell," it said; "good brethren all, and you, Brother Felix, pray for my soul. I am of the conviction that it is not good for man to live

alone. Being about to take unto myself a wife
and become a husband, I am constrained to sur-
render the Church. With this act, I cease being
a Father; but who knows what recompense the
future may not hold, so that, in time, I may become one again? God grant you a worthier suc-
cessor to

"PHILIPPE RENAUD."

As for Brother Felix, he laughed aloud. Once
alone, he straightway fell on his knees in prayer.
Long he remained thus motionless, and when at
last he arose, the silent walls heard him whisper
Renee's name.

———

On a Louisiana plantation, a white-haired old
man wept tears of sudden joy over the fair hand
of his son's wife.

"Now, Suzanne," cried Philippe, gayly; "now,
tell us about that object in life you would not dis-
close when I was your confessor!"

But Suzanne Renaud looked at him with grave,
sweet eyes:

"It was this," she said; "I knew from your gaze
and your words that you loved me. Like the

woman of old in the garden, I had determined
to tempt you.   I knew it would spoil your career,
perhaps, but I had determined to have you marry
me."

Again she smiled.

"That was my object in life, Philippe."

"Well, how did you accomplish your object,
my daughter?" asked the old man. "Did you
plan the elopement?"

There was a duet of hearty laughter from the
young people.

"The woods tell no tales," cried Philippe, with
his arm about his wife's slender waist. "It is
almost enough to know that it was I who proposed the marriage. It is entirely enough to
know that we have found happiness in the prospect of being together forever."

www.ingramcontent.com/pod-product-compliance
Lightning Source LLC
Chambersburg PA
CBHW030539270326
41927CB00008B/1446